O' TASTE AND SEE...

Chef Tracy Howard

Order this book online at www.trafford.com
or email orders@trafford.com

Most Trafford titles are also available at major online book retailers.

© Copyright 2011 Chef Tracy Howard.

All rights reserved. No part of this publication may be reproduced, stored in a retrieval system, or transmitted, in any form or by any means, electronic, mechanical, photocopying, recording, or otherwise, without the written prior permission of the author.

Printed in the United States of America.

ISBN: 978-1-4269-7278-2

Library of Congress Control Number: 2011914407

Trafford rev. 08/09/2011

 www.trafford.com

North America & international
toll-free: 1 888 232 4444 (USA & Canada)
phone: 250 383 6864 ♦ fax: 812 355 4082

Table of Contents

Introduction..2

Sunday Morning......................................5

Vegetarian..21

Poultry..35

Beef...59

Seafood..73

Desserts..87

Common Measurements........................110

F.Y.I..111

Introduction

O' Taste and See celebrates different types of quick and easy comfort foods that will make your every day meal special. As a professional chef I realize the importance of providing good tasty pleasing meals to your family. This book will do just that. Now you can cook meals like a chef in little or no time with my quick and easy recipes that brings a professional taste to ordinary foods. If your family is skeptical about trying a new dish, encourage them to ***"O' Taste and See"***.

Special Thanks

I thank God for being head of my life and for urging me to share the gifts and talents He has given me, which makes this book possible. I thank my parents, Martin, my children, Candy, Edna Curry, Pastor Michael Jackson, First Lady Kathy Jackson and the Tabernacle of Praise Family. Real special thanks to Sister C. Steed.

Credits:

Author and Chef: Tracy Howard

Typist: C. Steed

Photographers: Pina's Photography – Karla & Elena

Sunday Morning

Breakfast

Cold Cereal & Fresh Fruit

        1 Cup   Cereal of Choice

        Fresh Fruit

Choose your favorite cereal bowl; now choose your favorite cereal and fruit.

Pour the cereal into the bowl.

If you have a large fruit cut a portion and place in your cereal, eat the remaining fruit with your cereal. Pour milk over cereal and………. Enjoy!

Sausage Stuffed Pastry

2 lbs	ground sausage
1/3 c	onions
1/2 c	milk
1/2 c	butter
1/4 tsp	salt
1/4 tsp	pepper

Spray a skillet with oil spray. Heat skillet on medium heat.

Combine sausage, onions, salt, and pepper in skillet stirring for 10-15 minutes. While sausage is cooking, heat oven to 350°F. Remove sausage from heat, drain for 30 seconds, while sausage is draining. Prepare milk and butter in a saucepan, let simmer for 5 minutes. Remove pastry from freezer, add sausage to pastry, roll really tight, brush on milk and butter mixture with a pastry brush or paint brush. Place sausage roll on a cookie sheet, cook in oven for 15 to 20 minutes, when the pastry turns golden brown remove from oven, cut and serve. Yuummy!

Servings: 5

Blueberry Muffins with Boiled Egg

3/4 c	flour
1 tsp	baking powder
1/4 tsp	salt
3 1/4 tsp	sugar
1 tbs + 1tsp	chilled liquid eggs
1/2 c	milk
1 tbs + ¾ tsp	shortening
1 1/4 oz	fresh blueberries

In a mixing bowl combine all dry ingredients, blend with flat beater on low speed for 10 seconds. Combine eggs, milk and melted shortening. Add liquids to dry ingredients, mix on low speed for 15 seconds until blended (batter will still be lumpy). Carefully fold blueberries into the batter. Fill lined muffin tin with 1/2 cup of batter. Bake at 375°F for 20-25 minutes or until golden brown. Remove muffins from pan as soon as baked. While muffins are baking place egg in a pot of hot water boil for 20 minutes, remove from heat cool in cold water for 5 minutes, peel and serve.

Servings: 5

Belgian Waffles with Peach Topping and Whip Cream

5   Belgian Waffle (if you don't have a waffle maker, buy frozen)

Peach Topping:

1 can   Peaches

1 tsp   Vanilla Flavoring

¼ c   Water

2 tbs   Cornstarch

Whip Cream:

1 ¼ c   Heavy Whipping Cream

1 tsp   Sugar

In sauce pan combine peaches and vanilla, cook on medium high heat bring to a boil take ¼ cup of cold water add cornstarch whip add to peaches, stir until mixture is thick and bubbly, cook for 2 minutes longer.

To make whip cream –in a bowl whip cream for 4 minutes add sugar continue to whip until thick not stiff.

Place waffles in preheat 350°F oven to 15 minutes.

When ready to serve place raffle in a plate, spoon peach topping over waffle then top with whip cream sprinkle cinnamon on top.   Servings: 5

Hot Apple Slices over English Muffins

5 c	sliced apples
½ c	butter
½ tsp	cinnamon
½ tsp	nutmeg

Heat skillet at medium temperature, melt butter add sliced apples, cinnamon and nutmeg stirring for 5 to 10 minutes. Remove from heat when apples turn soft and serve English muffins.

Servings: 5

Corn Beef Hash

8 ¼ oz	cooked corn beef
6 ¾ oz	diced potatoes
1/3 c	diced yellow onions
¼ tsp	dill weed
½ c	olive oil
	Eggs (2 per person)

Chop corn beef mix in a bowl with diced onions, potatoes and dill weed. Heat skillet at medium temperature, pour in oil get oil hot, then pour in all ingredients, stir with a spatula, keep stirring and cook for about 30 minutes. Cook eggs 5 minutes before corn beef hash is done, 2 eggs per person. Mix eggs pour into heated skillet, cook eggs to your likening. Serve hash and eggs.

Servings: 5

Salmon Cake with Cream Caper Sauce

1- 14.75 oz can	pink salmon	2 ½ c	Olive oil
2 ¼ tsp	chopped yellow onions	1 ½ c	flour
2	eggs	¼ tsp	dill weed
¼ c	milk		

Combine salmon, onions, eggs, milk and spice in a bowl, put aside. Heat oil in a pan, once oil is hot, shape salmon mixture into patties and coat with flour, place in heated oil, cook on each side about 3 minutes drain on paper towel. Preheat oven to 350°F, place biscuits (I sometimes buy frozen biscuits) on cookie sheet bake for 13-17 minutes. While biscuits are baking prepare sauce.

Cream Caper Sauce:

1 c	water	1 c	milk
1 tbs	chicken base	3/8 tsp	Cajun spice
1/3 c	flour	1/3 c	margarine
			Capers

Melt margarine in heated skillet, remove from heat add flour and stir until smooth. In a pot on the stove heat milk and water, add chicken base stir with a wire whisk or fork stir sauce as necessary until smooth and thicken to the right consistency for about 15 minutes. Rinse capers in cold water and add to sauce, cook about 5 minutes. Biscuits should be done by now. Place salmon cake on plate spoon sauce over salmon, add biscuit. Now you're ready to eat.   Servings: 5

Vegetarian

Mediterranean Pasta

5 c	Whole Wheat Penne Rigate Pasta		1 c	Feta Cheese
2 ½ c	Sliced Black Olives		1c	Shredded Parmesan Cheese
2 1/2c	Diced Roman Tomatoes		dash	Fresh Ground Pepper
½ c	Fresh Basil		2	Pepperoncini
½ c	Fresh Garlic			Half Pita

Bring 3 ½ quarts of water to a rapid boil. Put pasta in water, cook uncovered stirring frequently for 10-15 minutes or until pasta is tender. Drain pasta, rinse pasta under cold water. On the side you will have your olives, diced tomatoes, chopped basil, chopped garlic, diced feta cheese, and parmesan cheese. Pour a dash of olive oil into hot skillet, add garlic sauté for a few seconds, and add tomatoes, olives, fresh oregano mix, cook for 30 seconds add pasta and feta cheese. Heat an additional 30 seconds when thoroughly heated, place into center of plate 2 pepperoncini in center of pasta, get pita and add your parmesan cheese on top of pasta. Serve and eat.

Servings: 5

Cajun Spice Bean Salad

1 stock	Fresh Romaine Lettuce chopped
3 c	Kernel Corn
3 c	Black Beans
¼ tsp	Cajun Spice
1/3 c	Balsamic Vinegar

Wash lettuce, open can of beans drain, rinse beans with cold water. In a bowl put chopped lettuce, corn and beans add Cajun spice, mix well then add balsamic vinegar. Mix well place on center of plate. Serve and eat.

Servings: 5

Fruit Medley

Seasonal Fresh Fruit

1 pint	Fresh Strawberries, sliced
1	Small Watermelon diced
1	Cantaloupe
1 pint	Fresh Blackberries

Prepare fruits, strawberries, melons. In the center of a plate place your lettuce for garnishing, place fruits around the plate. Serve and eat.

Servings: 5

Grilled Vegetables Night

3c	Tomatoes, sliced	2 tbs	Sweet basil oregano spice
1c	Small Button Mushrooms	1 tbs	Cajun Spice
1 oz	Sweet Bell Pepper		Zesty Italian Dressing
1 oz	Carrots, sliced		
1 oz	Red Onions, sliced		

Cut vegetables, they can be thick or thin your choice. Place all vegetables in a large bowl add spices and Italian dressing, let marinade for 30 minutes in refrigerator. Get grill hot, remove vegetables from refrigerator, spray vegetables with a cooking spray then place on grill. Grill each side 3-5 minutes, some vegetables may take a little longer on the grill. Serve

Servings: 5

Won Ton Wraps

1 pack	Won Ton Wraps			
3c	Oil			
1 1/2c	Finely shredded cabbage	**Sauce:**		
1 1/2c	Finely shredded red cabbage	1 c	Light Soy Sauce
1 1/2c	Shredded carrots	2 tbs	Honey
1 tbs	Cajun Spice	½ tsp	Ground ginger
1 tbs	Sweet Basil & Oregano Spice	½ tsp	All spice
¼ c	Olive Oil	½ tsp	cinnamon

Pour oil in a skillet, place skillet on medium heat, let oil get hot. Combine all the vegetables and spices in skillet, stir to mix well until vegetables get nice and tender or soft to your taste. In a saucepan combine all the ingredients for the sauce and cook slowly over medium heat until sauce thicken a little. In another skillet let oil get hot, get won ton wraps and fill with vegetables, fold in half, brush edge with water and press to seal, by now oil should be hot. Cook won ton wraps in oil for 2 minutes on each side until nice and golden. Place on plate and drizzle sauce over wraps. Serve and eat.   Servings: 5

Veggies in a String

15 oz	Spaghetti	3	Large Zucchini
1 ½	Sliced mushroom	2	Avocados
	Sliced Onions	2	Cloves of Garlic, crushed
	Cherry Tomatoes		
3	Large Yellow Squash		

A large pot of rapidly boiling water add salt and spaghetti, cook 10-12 minutes until tender, drain and return to pan. Have all vegetables washed and sliced. In skillet add 3 tablespoons of oil, heat on medium high heat add vegetables one by one, add spices of choice, stir and cook until vegetables are tender. Add pasta stir reduce heat to low. Serve.

Servings: 5

Poultry

Oven Fried Chicken

5	Medium Chicken Breasts
1/3c	Flour
1/3c	Dry Powder Milk
1 tbs	Garlic Salt
1 tbs	Black Pepper
1 tbs	Onion Powder
1/4c	Butter

Always wash meat in cold water. Combine flour, powder milk, garlic salt, black pepper and onion powder. In a plastic bag place chicken shake until breast is coated. Preheat oven to 350°F, place chicken in baking dish, melt ¼ cup butter, brush or spoon butter over chicken. Place meat in oven for 1 hour, remove chicken set aside. Take 2 slices of bread of choice add chicken to bread, serve with hot sauce. Old school chicken sandwich.

Servings: 5

BBQ Turkey Wings

3-5lbs	Large Turkey Wings	**BBQ Sauce:**	
2 tbs	Black Pepper	2 c	Ketchup
2 tbs	Garlic Salt	2 tbs	Mustard
2 tbs	Onion Salt	1/4c	Vinegar
1/2c	Brown Sugar		
1/3c	Light Soy Sauce		
1/3c	Worcestershire Sauce		

Rinse turkey wings under cold running water. Place wings in bowl add all your spices, put in refrigerator while preheating grill 10-20 minute. Prepare sauce, use a small sauce pan, pour ketchup, mustard, vinegar, sugar, soy sauce and worcesterhsire sauce, stir over low heat. Place turkey wings on grill cook wings 10-15 minutes on each side cook to 170°F for well done. Brush sauce on wings let grill for 2-5 minutes. Serve with baked potato. Plate up and eat.

Servings: 5

Asian Turkey Burger

1 1/2 lb	Ground Turkey	
1	Egg	
3 tsp	Worcestershire Sauce	
1 tsp	Black Pepper	
1 tsp	Salt	

Topping:

	Sliced Red Onions
	Sliced Tomatoes
1 1/2 c	Bean Sprouts

Teriyaki Sauce:

1/3 c	Teriyaki sauce
1/3 c	Worcestershire sauce
2 tbs	Brown sugar
1 tsp	Ginger powder
2 tbs	Garlic powder

Combine ground turkey, slightly beaten egg, worcestershire sauce, black pepper, and salt in a large bowl, mix and shape patties about ½ inch. Preheat grill, place buger on grill 4-6 minues until brown on each side. While burgers are grilling prepare teriyaki suace in a small sauce pan – soy sauce, brown sugar, ginger powder, garlic powder cook in medium heat until it boils, stir with whisk reduce to low heat, let simmer. Remove burger from grill set to side spoon sauce on roll, then place burger add onions, tomatoes and bean sprouts add more sauce over topping. Serve with fries.

Servings: 5

Citrus Almond Chicken

5	Boneless Chicken Breasts	**Citrus Sauce:**	
2 tbs	Salt	2 c	Orange Juice
2 tbs	Pepper	2 tbs	Sugar
1 1/2c	Mayonnaise	¼ c	Honey
2 pkgs	Sliced Almonds	Dash	Lime Juice
Dash	Lemon Juice		
¼ c	Coldwater		
2 tbs	Cornstarch		

Rinse chicken under cold water, place chicken on a cutting board; sprinkle seasoning add mayonnaise to chicken. Place almonds in a pan, roll chicken in almonds place on a baking sheet; place in oven preheated to 350°F, bake for 30-45 minutes depending on the size of the chicken. In a sauce pan combine orange juice, sugar, honey, lime juice, lemon juice; cook on medium heat stirring until smooth. Make a thickener by adding cold water to cornstarch. Add cornstarch to the citrus juices let simmer. Check chicken to see if it is done. Plate chicken add sauce, serve with yams and sugar snap peas.

Servings: 5

Chinese Bourbon Chicken

5	Chicken thighs	**Bourbon Sauce:**	
1 tbs	Garlic Salt	2 c	Water
1 tbs	Black Pepper	1 tbs	Paprika
1 tbs	Chicken base	¼ c	Bourbon
2 c	Flour	1 tbs	Garlic Cloves, chopped

Wash chicken under cold water add seasoning place in a bowl and set aside. Preheat 2 ½ cups of oil in a skillet on high heat. Roll chicken in flour and place in hot heat, cook on each side until well done. In a large skillet prepare bourbon sauce; pour water, add chicken base, bourbon and chopped garlic cook on low heat. Prepare thickener ¼ cup of cold water and cornstarch mix together; slowly whisk thickener into bourbon sauce add chicken let simmer for 10-15 minutes when done, plate and serve with fried rice.

Servings: 5

Orange Chicken Stir Fry

5	Skinless, boneless Chicken Breasts	**Orange Sauce:**	
2 tbs	Black Pepper	2 c	Orange juice
2 tbs	Salt	¼ c	Honey
1 tsp	Cinnamon	1/3 c	Sugar
3 tbs	Fresh Orange juice (squeezed and rind)	¼ c	Cold water
½ c	Sweet Teriyaki Sauce	2 tbs	Cornstarch

Wash and drain chicken breast, place in a bowl add black pepper, salt, cinnamon, orange juice, and sweet teriyaki sauce. Toss well place in refrigerator to marinate overnight or for 20 minutes. Preheat grill to medium high. Place chicken on skewers (if you use wood skewers, remember to presoak so that won't catch fire). Place chicken on grill, turning frequently cook for 7-12 minutes until chicken is tender. Prepare orange sauce – pour orange juice, add honey and sugar, cook on medium high heat bring to a boil, turn down to low heat, add cornstarch mixture stir until smooth. Brush orange sauce over chicken, let it grill for 2 minutes, remove from grill set aside. Preheat skillet for your stir fry pour 1/4 cup of oil, vegetables of choice, sugar, and light soy sauce cook for 5-7 minutes.

Servings : 5

Pork

Sweet and Sour Pork

3 ½ c	Diced Pork	**Paste:**	
1 tbs	Beef Base	¼ c	Cold Water
2 tsp	Light Soy Sauce	2 tbs	Cornstarch
2 tsp	Worcestershire Sauce		
2 tsp	Garlic Powder		

Vegetables:		**Sweet and Sour Sauce:**	
1/3 c	Oil	1 c	Pineapple juice
2 ½ c	Carrots	2 tbs	Sugar
2 ½ c	Celery	Dash	Salt
½ c	Onions	Dash	Pepper
		2 tbs	Light Soy Sauce
		1/3 c	Lemon Juice

In a skillet preheat 1/3 cup of oil, place rinsed pork in the skillet, add beef base, soy sauce, Worcestershire sauce, garlic powder, cover pan and cook on medium high heat for 30-40 minutes until meat is tender. When done drain oil off meat. Add your vegetables to hot boiling water to steam for 7-10 minutes, when vegetables are tender add to skillet. Reduce heat to medium low and simmer for a few minutes. In a sauce pan add pineapple juice, sugar, salt, pepper, soy sauce and lemon juice let cook on medium high heat until it starts to boil, add paste, cook on low until thicken, then pour half a cup of sauce to meat let reduce on low for a few minutes. If you desire you can add remaining sweet and sour sauce to rice and serve. Enjoy!

Servings: 5

BBQ Baby Back Ribs with Brandy

2	Slabs of baby back ribs		

Marinating Sauce:		**BBQ Sauce:**	
	Dill weed	1 can	Pureed Apricots
	Garlic salt	1 ½ c	Ketchup
	Onion salt	¼ c	Mustard
	Black pepper	1/3 c	Vinegar
	Paprika	½ c	Brown Sugar
	Dash of Cajun spice	Dash	Crushed Hot Peppers
3 c	brandy	3 caps	Brandy

Marinate meat in brandy and spices over night. Preheat grill to medium high, cook meat about 30 minutes (15 minutes on each side)

Cook BBQ sauce in a sauce pan on medium heat, bring to rapid boil, add brandy near the end and let simmer and reduce for 20 minutes.

Ribs remain on grill, brush sauce on the ribs let ribs grill an additional 2-3 minutes.

Hawaiian Kabobs

2 c	Diced Pork	**Hawaiian Sauce:**	
1/3 c	Light Soy Sauce	2 c	Ketchup
3 tsp	Black pepper	½ c	Pineapple Juice
1 tbs	Salt	1/3 c	Teriyaki Sauce
1	Fresh Pineapple (cut in cubes)	1/3 c	Sugar
½ c	Cherry Tomatoes	¼ c	Vinegar

Paste:

¼ c	Water
2 tbs	Cornstarch

Wash pork under cold water, place pork in a bowl add pepper, salt, soy sauce. Preheat grill to medium high. Cut pineapple and tomatoes and set aside. Place pork on skewers (if using wood skewers presoak in water) cook on grill 7-12 minutes on each side turning frequently. On the other skewers put tomatoes, pineapples because they tend to cook faster than the meat. When the meat is done put meat on the vegetable skewers. In sauce pan add ketchup, pineapple juice, teriyaki sauce, sugar and vinegar boil on medium heat when it start to boil add paste, then boil until thickens. Brush Hawaiian sauce on pork grill for 2 minutes. Serve with white rice.

Servings: 5

Smothered Ham Hocks with Cornbread

3 lbs	Ham hocks	**Gravy:**	
2 tbs	Thyme	3 c	Cold Water
1 tsp	White Pepper	2 tsp	Beef Base
1 tsp	Salt	1 tsp	Garlic Powder
2	Large Onions (chopped)	2	Sliced Onions
4	Whole Carrots	**Roux:**	
	Bay Leaves	1/3 c	Flour
		¼ c	Melted Butter

In a large pot add 2 quarts of water bring to a boil; add hocks, salt, white pepper, onions, carrots and bay leaves continue boiling for 2 hours or until meat is tender. In a skillet place 3 cups of cold water add beef base and garlic powder and onions. In a skillet make roux, melt butter remove from add flour stir until smooth, then add roux to gravy cook on medium high heat stirring occasionally 5-10 minutes, add hocks to gravy let simmer for 15-20 minutes. Serve with Cornbread.

Servings: 5

Beef

Zesty Beef Tips

4 lb	Beef Tips
1 tsp	Garlic Salt
1 tsp	Black Pepper
3 tbs	Worcestershire Sauce
3	Fresh Oranges squeezed
3	Fresh Lemons squeezed
1	Fresh Limes squeezed

Rinse beef tips in cold water, place meat in a bowl. Add spices, pinch of ginger, Worcestershire sauce, squeezed fresh fruits, marinate for 30 minutes. Cut fresh vegetables of your choice into medium portions. Preheat grill to medium high. Place meat and vegetables on metal skewers, place on grill until meat is tender about 15-20 minutes continue to turn meat. If meat is not tender enough cook in a skillet a few minutes longer. Plate up serve and eat.

Servings: 5

Beef and Broccoli

2 lbs	Diced Beef
2 tbs	Beef Base
1 tbs	Black Pepper
2 tbs	Garlic Powder
1 tbs	Onion Powder
3 tbs	Light Soy Sauce
2 tbs	Worcestershire Sauce
5 c	Steamed Fresh Broccoli

Rinse diced beef under cold water. In a large skillet, preheated to medium heat, add oil to cover skillet heat about 2 minutes. Place diced beef in skillet add base, pepper, garlic powder, onion powder, soy sauce and Worcestershire sauce, mix well, cover pan cook about 1 and one-half hour (keep checking) when beef gets tender reduce heat add 1/3 cup of flour; mix with a fork until juice thickens; simmer for about 15 minutes add steamed broccoli . Plate and serve.

Servings: 5

Pulled Roast Beef Sandwich w/ Shiraz Cabernet Gravy

	Left over roast beef (from Sunday's dinner)
	Salt
	Pepper
	Garlic
2 tbs	Cornstarch
¼ c	Cabernet Wine
	Black Pepper

Cabernet Gravy:

1 c	Cold water
1 tbs	Beef base

To make gravy add wine to beef base and cold water, cook on medium high heat. In a cup or small container mix cornstarch with 1/3 cup of cold water to make a thickener; add thickener to the beef base and wine mixture; turn to low heat let simmer allow liquids to reduce. Pull beef and place in gravy. Cut a sub roll in half place pulled pork on roll top with gravy.

Servings: 5

Green Olive Burger

2 lbs	Ground beef		Topping:
2	Eggs		Blue Cheese Dressing
Dash	Salt		Sliced Lettuce
Dash	Pepper		Sliced Tomatoes
2tbs	Red Hot Sauce		Sliced Onions
2tbs	Worcestershire Sauce	1/2c	Sliced green olives

Combine ingredients in bowl- beef, beaten eggs, spices, and mix well; shape into patties about ½ inch thick. Heat skillet on medium high heat when skillet is hot place patties in skillet and pan broil for about 7-10 minutes per each side. Take your burger rolls pour a little blue cheese dressing on each roll then burger, lettuce, tomatoes, onions and sliced green olives.

Plate and serve. Servings: 5

Hickory Smoked Steak

5	Steaks (steak of your choice)	5/8 tsp	Worcestershire Sauce
Dash	White Pepper	1/3 c	Chopped Garlic
Dash	Salt	1 1/2c	Sliced Fresh Mushrooms
5/8 tsp	Light Soy Sauce	1 1/2c	Beef Broth

Preheat grill, grill steak on medium high for 7-12 minutes on each side. Prepare gravy- water, beef broth, in a saucepan on medium high, bring to a boil, add cap full of mesquite flavoring. Make a thickener with cold water and cornstarch add using a wire whisk, add fresh garlic and mushrooms. Remove steaks from grill place in gravy let simmer for about 10 minutes. Plate and serve.

Servings: 5

Lamb Chops in Sweet Chili Sauce

10	Lamb Chops (2 per person)
Dash	Black Pepper
Dash	Salt
1/3 c	Light Soy Sauce
1/2c	Sweet Chili Sauce
4	Cloves

This lamb you will want to marinate overnight to get that great taste. Rinse lamb, place in a small bowl add black pepper, salt, soy sauce, put cloves in meat, add chili sauce put in refrigerator. The next day preheat grill to medium high heat, place lamb chops on grill let cook for 5-7 minutes per side. If not tender put meat in skillet and simmer for 10 minutes on low heat. Prepare a salad. Plate and serve.

Servings: 5

Seafood

Blacken Salmon

5	Fresh Salmons
	Dill weed
1	Stick of butter
1/3 c	Lemon Juice

Rinse salmon under cold water. In a large iron skillet melt butter and lemon juice on medium-high heat. Season salmon with spices on each side, place salmon in skillet, cook on each side for 7-10 minutes. Remember the thickness of the salmon, cook salmon until it turns dark on each side, steam asparagus until tender.   Plate and serve. Serve with Steamed Asparagus

Servings: 5

Clams over Spaghetti

25	Fresh Clams (5 per person)	1/3 c	Diced Tomatoes
15 oz	Spaghetti	½ tsp	Pepper
1/3 c	Butter	½ tsp	Salt
2	Shallots, finely chopped	3 tbs	Fresh Chopped Cilantro
3	Fresh chopped Garlic cloves		Handful Fresh Basil

Soak clams in salt water for 20-25 minutes; while clams are soaking in a large pot of boiling salt water add spaghetti for 10-12 minutes or according to package directions until tender. Drain spaghetti into a large skillet heat butter over medium heat add shallots, garlic and tomatoes. Let simmer for 5 minutes, drain water off the clams run under cold water, add clams to skillet, fresh basil, lemon juice and spices. Turn with tongs let simmer for few minutes until clams open. Place spaghetti in center of plate, remove clams and place on top of spaghetti with a spoon, and sprinkle fresh cilantro. Serve and eat.

Servings: 5

Crab Spring Rolls

1pkg	Egg Roll Wraps	1/4c	Chopped Garlic
1 lb	Crab Flakes (imitation)	3 1/2c	Oil
1pkg	Green Cabbage and Carrots Mix	1/3c	Light Soy Sauce
3c	Bean Sprouts	2 1/2c	Flour

In a skillet combine cabbage and carrots mix, bean sprouts, add garlic, soy sauce cook on medium heat until vegetables get tender, turn 2 times and remove from stove, add crab (should be in pieces). Place filling diagonally on wrap. Have a small bowl of water to put on edges according to package directions to seal the wraps. Measure flour in a bowl to coat wraps. In a large skillet heat oil on medium high until oil is very hot, place a few rolls in hot oil flat side down turning occasionally until golden brown 3-4 minutes each side, drain. Place wrap on plate with sweet chili sauce on the side.

Servings: 5

Fish in Foil

5	Tilapia Fillets		Fresh Basil Loaves
¼ tsp	Black Pepper		Butter
	Fresh Bay Leaves		Pinch Smoked Salt
	Fresh Parsley		

Use baking sheet and 5 pieces of foil for fish. Rinse fish under cold water one by one, place fish in foil; add smoked salt pepper and fresh bay leaves, fresh parsley, fresh basil leaves. Preheat oven to 350°F, place fish in oven for 20-25 minutes. Plate fish and serve with wild rice on the side.

Servings: 5

Seafood Medley

10	Large scallops (2 each)		
5	Large Catfish Filets		Chilled Tartar Sauce:
10	Large Shrimps (2 each)	1c	Hot & Spicy mayonnaise
1c	Flour	1/2c	Dill Relish
1c	Corn Meal	1tbs	Soy Sauce
1tbs	Dill weeds or Spice of your choice	1tbs	Worcestershire Sauce
		1tbs	Lemon Juice

Rinse all your seafood under cold water. In a bowl put all dry ingredients, take scallops, fish, shrimp, cover with dry spices. Heat oil in large skillet on medium high heat until nice and hot, add scallops – fry on each side for 3 minutes. Preheat oven to 300°F; place fried scallops and shrimp on baking sheet put in oven to stay hot. Fry fish 5-7 minutes on each side, take off stove place on baking sheet put in oven. In bowl put mayonnaise, relish, soy sauce, Worcestershire sauce and lemon juice beat with a fork or wire whisk, let set in refrigerator for 5-10 minutes. Plate and serve.

Servings: 5

Steamed Mahi-Mahi

Lemon Butter Sauce:

5	Large Mahi-Mahi	1/2c	Butter
½ tsp	Black Pepper	1/4c	Lemon Juice
1/2tsp	Salt	1 tsp	Parsley flake

Marinade for Fish:

		1 tsp	Worcestershire Sauce
1 1/2c	Brown sugar	1tsp	Soy Sauce
½ stck	Melted Butter	1/2tsp	Salt
1 1/2c	Soy Sauce	½ tsp	Black Pepper
Small Rival Steamer or baking sheet		¼ tsp	Garlic Salt

Marinade fish for 20 minutes. If you have a steamer put water in steamer, remove fish from marinade put in steamer for 20 minutes or if you don't have a steamer, place on baking sheet for 20-25 minutes until tender or reach 165°F temperature, well done. In skillet braise sliced squash, onions and spices until tender. To make lemon butter sauce, place all ingredients in a sauce pan, cook on medium heat for 5-7 minutes. Plate fish top with sauce, serve on the side squash with sliced onions

Servings: 5

Desserts

Avocado Ice Cream Pie with Strawberry Sauce

3	Avocadoes	**Sauce:**	
3c	Fresh Vanilla Ice Cream	1/4c	Water
1	Oreo Pie Crust	1/4c	Fresh Sliced Strawberries
1/3c	Sugar		

Avocadoes should start turning soft or really ripe. Put peeled avocadoes in mixer bowl using wire whip turn mixer speed to 5 and whip for 3-5 minutes until lump free and getting soft. Add ice cream to avocadoes, mix well for 3 minutes until creamy and soft, and pour ice cream mixture into crust, freeze about 1 hour. In a sauce pan add water, sliced strawberries and sugar cook on high heat. Slowly turn heat down to low and stir until strawberries and sugar are dissolved completely. Get ¼ cup of water add ¼ cup of cornstarch, mix together then add to sauce to thicken. Let set for 30 minutes. When ready to serve take pie out of freezer cut pie place on a plate, drizzle strawberry sauce over pie. Enjoy!

Servings: 5

Banana Pudding

1 pkg	Instant Banana Pudding Mix
2 c	Milk

Cream Filling:

1 1/4c	Heavy Cream
1 tsp	Vanilla Flavoring
1 tsp	Sugar
	Vanilla Wafers
1	Banana

Prepare pudding according to directions on box. Place pudding in refrigerator. Now whip heavy cream on high speed for 2-3 minutes, turn speed down to 5-6 add vanilla and sugar stop whipping when peaks form. In glasses go layer by layer, sliced banana first, then pudding, then cream mixture, repeat layers, once you get to the top sprinkle crushed cookies on top. Yummmm!

Servings: 5

Chocolate Dessert Cups

5	Chocolate Dessert Shells	**Whipped Cream:**	
1 pint	Fresh Strawberries	1 1/4 c	Heavy Cream
1 pint	Fresh Raspberries	1 pkg	Equal
1 pint	Fresh Blackberries	1 tsp	Vanilla Extract
		3 caps	Kahlua

Chocolate Syrup:

¼ c	Oil
1/3 c	Chocolate Chips

Wash fruit, drain set aside. In a large bowl whip heavy cream on low speed for a few minutes, turn up speed gradually add sugar, vanilla extract and kahlua, whip rapidly until cream is stiff . For chocolate syrup pour oil in a sauce pan place on low heat, when oil gets hot add chocolate chips, stir until smooth remove from heat. Place fresh fruits in chocolate dessert shells, spoon on whipped cream drizzle with syrup.

Servings: 5

Pina Colada Cupcakes

1 box	Yellow Cake Mix

Frosting:

1 stick	Butter or margarine softened
1 1/2c	Powder Sugar
1/4c	Pina Colada Mix
1/4c	Jose Cuervo Especial
1 can	Chopped Pineapples
	Toasted Coconut Flakes
	Whole Cherries

Prepare cake mix according to package directions. Frosting, place butter in mixer bowl using flat beater turn mixer to speed 4 and beat for 30 seconds, stop mixer add powder sugar, add vanilla flavoring, pina colada mix as well as Jose Cuervo turn speed to 2 and beat for 30 seconds, stop and scrape bowls. Turn speed to 4 and beat 2 minutes or until fluffy. Frost cupcakes with frosting. Brown coconut in oven preheated to 350°F for 2-5 minutes, garnish with pineapples and coconut. Top with cherry. Serve and eat.

Servings: 5

Orange Spice Cake

1 box	Spice cake mix	**Topping:**	
3	Eggs	1 c	Orange juice
1 1/3 c	Water		Fresh Orange Rind
1/3 c	Oil	1/3 c	Sugar
		1 tsp	Cinnamon
Paste:		1 tsp	Nutmeg
¼ c	Water		
2 tbs	Cornstarch		

Prepare spice cake according to direction on box, bake in a 13x9 cake pan at 350°F for 33-36 minutes. When done remove from oven and let cool.

Topping: In a sauce pan pour orange juice, add the grated rinds, sugar, cinnamon and nutmeg, cook on medium heat until mixture boils, reduce heat to low add paste stir until smooth, let simmer, remove from heat and let cool.

Spread topping on cake.

Servings: 5

Mango in Butter

5 c	Dried Mangoes
4 oz	Butter
¼ tsp	Cinnamon
¼ tsp	Nutmeg
1/3 c	Sugar

In a large sauce pan melt butter over medium heat, stir in mangoes, stir constantly, add cinnamon, nutmeg, and sugar, reduce heat to low and simmer 7-10 minutes, keep turning until tender. Place mangoes on a plate let cool before adding cool whip.

Servings: 5

Fried Dough

1 can	Biscuit dough
¼ tsp	Cinnamon
¼ tsp	Sugar

In a skillet heat oil on medium high heat until you hear oil pop. Place dough in skillet cook until it floats about 3-4 minutes. When done drain, in a bowl combine cinnamon and sugar, sprinkle over fried dough.

Servings: 5

Sweet Potato Coconut Crunch

3	Yams (medium)	2	Eggs
4 oz	Butter	2 cans	Condensed Milk
½ c	Sugar	¼ c	Coconut Flakes
1 tsp	Cinnamon	2	9" Pie Shells
1 tsp	Nutmeg	½ c	Cereal of your Choice
1 tsp	Vanilla		

Boil yams for 30 minutes until they become soft, peel yams place in bowl, mix on medium speed for 3 minutes, add remaining ingredients, butter, sugar, cinnamon, nutmeg, vanilla , eggs, and condensed milk, mix well for 3-4 minutes on speed 6, fold in coconut. pour into pie shell. Place pies in oven preheated to 350°F bake for 1 hour, after an hour check doneness of pie by inserting a knife into center of the pie, if knife comes out clean pie is done remove from oven sprinkle cereal crumbs over pie, return to oven and bake for 2-3 minutes.

Servings: 5

Strawberry Shortcake

2 c	All purpose Flour	**Topping:**		
1 tbs	Baking Powder	1 c	Water
tsp	Salt	1 c	Fresh Strawberries
1/3 c	Shortening	1/3 c	Sugar
¾ c	Milk		

Cool Whip

Combine flour, baking powder and salt cut in shortening until mixture resembles coarse crumbs, make a well in the center add milk all at once, stir with fork until dough clings together, use scoop #24 to drop dough onto cookie sheet. Preheat oven to 350°F bake for 10-12 minutes.

Sauce: Bring water, strawberries and sugar to a boil rapidly on medium high heat., add cornstarch paste until thicken, spoon over biscuits and top with cool whip.

Servings: 5

Chocolate Covered Strawberries

2 pints	Strawberries
¼ c	oil
¼ c	Chocolate Chips

Wash strawberries, dry strawberries on a cloth. In a sauce pan pour oil, let it get hot (about 2 minutes) then add chips turn heat to low stir chocolate chips until smooth. Dip strawberries in chocolate, set aside until strawberries are dry about 1 minute. Place on plate, serve and eat.

Servings: 5

Cheesecake in a Glass

8 oz	Soften Cream Cheese
¼ c	Vanilla Extract
1/3 c	Powdered Sugar

Whip cream cheese in a bowl for about 2-3 minutes, add vanilla and powdered sugar, whip again for about 20 seconds, until liquid is absorbed and mixture forms peaks. Spoon cream cheese mixture into 5 glasses let chill in refrigerator for 30 minutes, add fruit of choice.

Servings: 5

Common Measurements

1 tablespoon = 3 teaspoons

1 cup = 16 tablespoons

1 pint = 2 cups

1 quart = 2 pints

Scoops Size	**Cups**	**Ounces**
#5 scoop	2/3 c	6 oz
#8 scoop	½ c	4-5 oz
#10 scoop	3/8 c	3-4 oz
#12 scoop	1/3 c	2 ½-3 oz
#16 scoop	¼ c	2-2 ¼ oz
#20 scoop	3 1/5 tbs	1 ¾-2 oz
#30 scoop	2 1/5 tbs	1-1 ½ oz

F.Y.I.
(For Your Information)

Hand washing – Wash hand using antibacterial soap under very warm water for 20 seconds.

Thawing Food – Thaw food in the refrigerator or under running cold water at 70°F temperature or lower, not on the counter. Store raw food on the lowest shelf to prevent them from dripping or splashing on other foods.

Preventing Cross Contamination: Never cut meat on a cutting board without cleaning and washing after each use, as well your knife and other kitchen tools. Not just for meats but any kind of food.

Cook Food to the Right Temperature: Always cook foods at the right temperature and keep a thermometer handy to check the temperature of foods.

Keep It Clean: Keep the spot where you are cooking clean so no foreign objects get in the food.

Danger Zone: Danger zone temperature for cold foods is 41 – 135. On all cold foods temperature needs to be 40 or lower. Never let meat sit out use it right away or put back in refrigerator.

How to Check Temperature

To make sure the food you are cooking has reached the right temperature; you must know how to take the temperature correctly. Pick a thermometer with a probe that is the right size for the food. Check the temperature in the thickest part of the food and take at least two readings in different locations. It is good to have two different thermometers one for food and the other for your refrigerator, which should stay in the refrigerator at all times.

Temperatures and cooking requirement of specific foods:

Poultry – Including whole or ground chicken, turkey or duck minimum internal temperature is 170°F (74°C) for well done for 15 seconds.

Ground Meat – Including beef, pork and other meats minimum internal temperature 160°F (68°C) for well done for 15 seconds.

Lamb, veal and roast of pork- minimum internal temperature 160°F (63°C) for well done for 15 seconds.

Seafood – including fish, shellfish and crustaceans minimum temperature 155°F (63°C) for well done for 15 seconds.

Commercially processed, ready to eat food that will be hot held for service (cheese sticks and deep-fried vegetables) 135°F (57°C).

Fruits, vegetables, pasta, rice, grains and beans that will be hot held at 135°F (57°C).

Hi! I am Chef Tracy Howard….

For over thirty years I have had the joy of making great meals as a chef cooking for hundreds or making a loving meal at home, cooking has been my passion. I am from Rochester, New York. Growing up in the upper New York region greatly influenced my style of cooking.

Now I live in Las Vegas, Nevada a melting pot of all the great foods of the world. I love discovering new things and an even greater challenge is making the everyday meal special. O Taste and See is comfort food with a twist. As a mother preparing meals to keep my family happy as well as keeping the menu fresh at work is always a challenge. Using regional and seasonal foods unique to your area will add flair to your dishes. I love watching people's eyes light up when I can make their every day special. So here's to you, O Taste and See the best to you and yours.

Great meals to you and thank you.

www.ingramcontent.com/pod-product-compliance
Lightning Source LLC
Chambersburg PA
CBHW041118300426
44112CB00002B/20